WORKING PAPER

Locating Adaptive Learning: The Situated Nature of Adaptive Learning in Organizations

Marcie J. Tyre
Eric von Hippel

May 1993   WP # 90-93

INTERNATIONAL CENTER
FOR RESEARCH ON
THE MANAGEMENT OF TECHNOLOGY

Massachusetts Institute of Technology
Sloan School of Ma

The International Center for Research
on the Management of Technology

Locating Adaptive Learning: The Situated Nature
of Adaptive Learning in Organizations

Marcie J. Tyre
Eric von Hippel

May 1993   WP # 90-93

Sloan WP# BPS 3568-93

Sloan School of Management
Massachusetts Institute of Technology
38 Memorial Drive, E56-390
Cambridge, MA   02139-4307

Acknowledgement

The research reported upon in this paper was funded by the International Center for Research on the Management of Technology at the MIT Sloan School of Management and the MIT Leaders for Manufacturing Program The authors gratefully acknowledge this support

ABSTRACT

This paper describes the nature of adaptive learning processes in organizations. We examine the process of problem solving around new manufacturing equipment following field tests and early factory use We find that adaptation is a situated process, in that different organizational settings (1) contain different kinds of clues about the underlying issues, (2) expose learners to different ideas, and (3) offer different resources for generating and analyzing information. Consequently, actors frequently must move in an iterative fashion between different organizational settings before they can identify the causal underpinnings of a problem and select suitable solutions.

This finding adds an additional dimension to the literature on adaptive learning processes, which currently focuses almost exclusively on social knowledge exchange (via discussion, argument, and collaborative "sensemaking"). We propose that theories of adaptive learning should also take into account how actors (both collectively and individually) use their surroundings to understand events, and how these surroundings affect the social interactions that unfold.

Errors encountered in the process of trying new policies, technologies, or behaviors are a major source of learning and improvement in organizations. As Hedberg (1981:4) argues, "attempts to act expose the conditions for acting, causal relations...are gradually untangled." However, despite its importance, we have only partial understanding of the processes underlying such "untangling".

Existing research focuses on the social or interpersonal nature of adaptive learning in organizations. It points to the importance of "processes like discussion and persuasion, and ...[of] relationships like trust and antagonism" for making sense of ambiguous events (March and Olsen, 1975:166). Even when the focus is an observable physical object, such as a broken machine, the adaptation process is described as a social one "that begins as well as ends in a communal understanding of the machine" among actors with different experiences and different kinds of knowledge (Brown and Duguid,1991:44). Such communal processes are variously described in terms of social sensemaking (Weick, 1979), story telling (Brown and Duguid, 1991), collaborative inquiry (Argyris and Schon, 1978), collaborative diagnosis (Cicourel, 1990), inter-entity knowledge relationships (Ching, Holsapple and Whinston, 1992), and confrontation and contest (Cicourel,1990:139). The importance of such collaborative processes stems from the fact that no one person embodies the requisite knowledge to comprehend complex organizational problems, or the requisite variety to clarify equivocal issues. Thus, collaboration is seen as "the essence of what distinguishes [organizational learning] from entity learning" (Ching et al., 1992:293-4); or "the distinctive feature of organization level information activity" (Daft and Lengel, 1984:285).

In this paper, we report on a study of adaptive learning in the process of introducing and debugging new process equipment in a manufacturing environment. By adaptive learning, we mean both the investigation and subsequent changes in behaviors, technologies, or beliefs undertaken in response to negative feedback. In this sense, adaptive learning has both a behavioral component (changes in performance) and a cognitive aspect (changes in understanding) (Fiol and Lyles, 1985).

We find that adaptive learning in response to machine problems does not always involve collaborative interactions. Instead, we observe that learners often rely on other aspects of their physical settings to "untangle" the reasons for unexpected errors and to explore the alternatives available. Specifically, the events, procedures, technical systems, and daily routines embedded in a given setting provide learners with both specific clues as to the nature of the problem (or solution), and tools or resources to aid investigation and solution work. This means that learning is *situated* in the sense that *where* activities take place (and not just who is talking to whom) matters. The physical setting partly determines what actors can do, what they know, and what they can learn. [1]

Moreover, because different settings provide different opportunities for learning, activities in different physical settings have a cumulative quality: progress in one setting often makes it possible to better utilize clues or resources located in a different physical domain. Thus, learners often have to shift iteratively between several settings (e.g., lab and plant) before they reach an understanding of the underlying problem and possible alternatives.

We argue that if adaptive learning in organizations is a situated process, then the physical settings that contain it deserve greater attention from scholars and managers. The skills and knowledge of people in organizations are often dependent on their physical settings -- skills reside in the machines they use, the physical cues they rely on to perform daily routines, their intimate knowledge of how to exploit or interpret local idiosyncrasies, and so on (cf Lave, 1988; Scribner, 1984; Suchman, 1987). Seeing, touching, and manipulating are obviously important avenues for improving understanding, just as hearing and explaining are; yet, they are nearly overlooked in the organizational literature on adaptive learning[1].

METHODOLOGY

Data for this study were gathered from two projects involving the introduction of new production machines into factory contexts. The introduction and subsequent adaptation of new production equipment in the manufacturing plant provides a rich context in which to study organizational adaptive learning. Unexpected problems are common, and adaptation is important -- both for developing new technical solutions, and for clarifying previously undefined cause and effect relationships (Rosenberg, 1982; Leonard-Barton, 1988). Further, interaction among multiple organizational actors (principally manufacturing engineers who work in the lab, and users who work in the manufacturing context) has been shown to be important for diagnosing and resolving errors with new process equipment (Tyre and Hauptman, 1992).

Our research approach has several distinctive features. First, following Van de Ven and others (Van de Ven, Angle and Poole, 1989; Van de Ven and Polley, 1992), we focus on specific events as the unit of analysis. The "events" of interest are errors or problems discovered with new equipment, and subsequent adaptive activities. Specifically, for each problem that users encountered in trying to apply new process equipment, we examine the associated actions,

---

1 It is worth noting that several scholars in related fields have recently focused on the importance of seeing -- in several senses -- for improving design processes. Schon and Wiggins (1992) describe the multiple "kinds of seeing" involved in the interaction between a designer (e g , an architect) and her physical design (e g , a drawing). Leonard-Barton (1991) shows that examination of a physical object (e.g. a prototype of a new product) can sometimes be a powerful vehicle for meaningful communication among designers and users

perceptions, and interactions. This differs from the more traditional foc
learning inputs and outcomes at the level of the organization or suborganization
(e.g. Levinthal and March, 1981; Lounamaa and March, 1987). Further,
following Lave (1984), Scribner (1984), and others, we paid specific attention to
how ideas or information were generated or gathered: in what places, events, or
routines were these things situated, who identified them, and under what
circumstances did people or information move among different organizational
settings.

Research Setting

The new process machines selected for study were currently in use in two
unrelated factories of a large electronics manufacturer. The machines had been
developed independently in two separate in-house labs. Both of the machines are
used in automated assembly of complex circuit boards; the first (called a solder
paste profiler) automatically inspects the solder dabs that are applied to the board
prior to component placement. The second machine (called a component placer)
automatically places electronic components in the desired positions on the board.
Each machine was eventually described as successful by users and engineers, and
has since been replicated for use in other factories.

Sample of Adaptations Studied

Our sample contains 27 adaptations undertaken in response to users'
problems with the new technology (fifteen affecting the placer, and twelve
affecting the profiler) This represents all of those changes made (to the new
technology, related procedures, or beliefs) that met the following criteria. First,
all changes were made after the equipment was installed in the production plant.
Second, changes were undertaken in response to problems recognized by users.
Third, data on the actions taken to investigate and resolve the problem were

available via verbal report, direct observation, and/or plant records.

Problem symptoms included machine malfunction, unsatisfactory processing of parts, or user dissatisfaction with convenience or efficiency. Adaptation typically consisted of modifications to hardware or software elements of the machine or (and) to users' procedures, as well as adjustments in engineers' and users' beliefs about cause-and-effect relationships.

Data Collection

Data on machine problems and adaptive activities were collected through interviews with both the user of each machine (the process technician primarily in charge of the machine at the factory) and the engineer (the advanced manufacturing engineer primarily responsible for designing and debugging the machine). At both field sites, engineers maintained primary responsibility for diagnosing and resolving problems that occurred in the field throughout the test period.

For each problem in the sample, respondents were asked to describe both the problem identification and problem-solving processes in detail. A number of methods were used to elicit accurate recall of events. A primary interview question was, "Please describe changes that you made to the machine (or its surroundings, or techniques for using it) after its introduction." We then asked respondents to describe the problems that triggered each of these changes, and the actions taken to resolve problems. This was followed by more detailed probing (e.g., "Why did you call A (or do B) at that point?"). This provided a critical-event history of each problem that could later be traced.

Initial interviews were conducted on-site where respondents could refer to contemporary logbooks and could demonstrate the problems they described. Interviews lasted from three to six hours, including plant tours. Respondents were interviewed both separately and, subsequently, together. Follow-up questions were discussed in additional face-to-face meetings, and by telephone and electronic mail.

Field notes were taken by both authors and coding of responses was done by both authors and compared for consistency. Disagreements were discussed until consensus was reached; when ambiguity persisted, additional data were gathered.

Several factors served to mitigate concerns about data accuracy given our mainly retrospective approach. First, machine problems and associated changes were considered both important and noteworthy events by users and engineers; this facilitated recall. Second, our reconstruction of events and interactions depended on independent descriptions by different respondents (the engineer and the user). Accuracy of recall appeared to be very high, as indicated by the high degree of agreement between users and engineers on the list of changes made and the actions leading to those changes. Where we found disagreement, we discussed it with respondents (often in joint meetings with both users and engineers) to discover the reason. Third, wherever possible we used specific memorable events or milestones that were available from plant records (such as the date when a new machine part was ordered) to serve as a memory aid or anchor. We frequently asked respondents to check lab notebooks or plant production records. Finally, while it is possible that some of the actions taken as part of the adaptation process (e.g. visits to the plant or the lab) had been forgotten, it is less likely that events which did not take place were later added in respondents' memories Therefore we feel that any bias introduced through forgetting is likely to be conservative relative to our main findings.

RESULTS

A striking feature of the adaptation process was the use of different physical settings for responding to a single problem. In most of the cases studied, engineers needed to investigate the same issue in two different locations (the plant and the lab). They often shifted repeatedly between locations before they felt they could understand and resolve the problem.

The use of different physical settings is illustrated in the following example. During the early field tests with the profiler, users found that the machine was providing incorrect readings of the height of solder dabs. Users informed the advanced manufacturing engineer, who went to the plant to observe the machine and to run some diagnostic tests. Next, the engineer returned to her lab to analyze the data. Results showed the need for further investigation, so the engineer again went back to the plant for further tests and observation. These tests revealed the source of the problem (reflection off the board surface was interfering with the machine's ability to locate the board surface). While still at the plant, the engineer implemented and tested programming changes to reduce the problem. Users quickly noticed a significant improvement in accuracy.

In the example above, the principal problem solver (the advanced manufacturing engineer) used the plant and the lab as complementary settings for learning about the problem. Over the course of this relatively simple issue, the engineer relocated adaptive activities three times, as shown in Figure 1:

8

FIGURE 1: ITERATION BETWEEN LAB AND PLANT

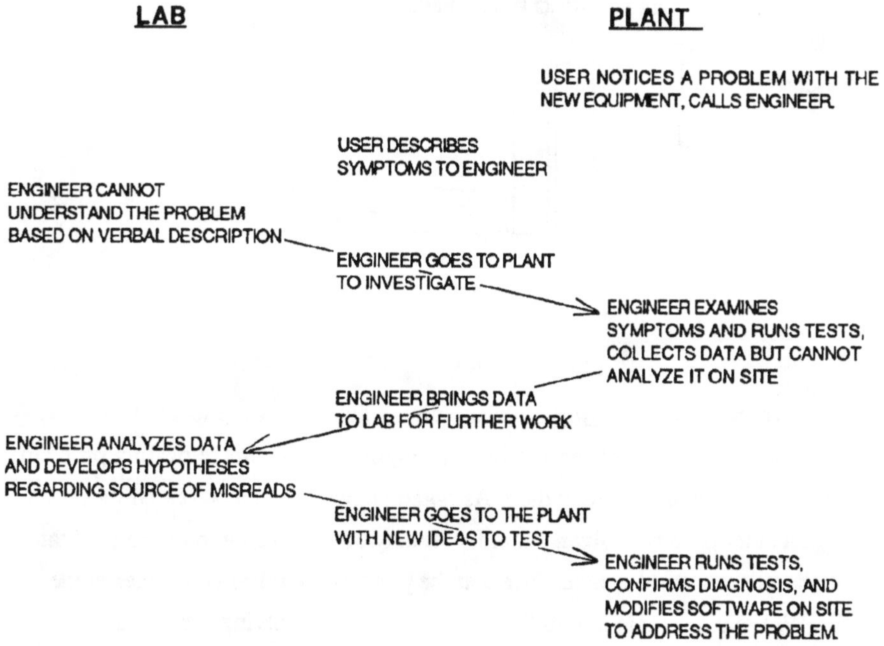

LAB   **PLANT**

USER NOTICES A PROBLEM WITH THE
NEW EQUIPMENT, CALLS ENGINEER.

USER DESCRIBES
SYMPTOMS TO ENGINEER

ENGINEER CANNOT
UNDERSTAND THE PROBLEM
BASED ON VERBAL DESCRIPTION

ENGINEER GOES TO PLANT
TO INVESTIGATE

ENGINEER EXAMINES
SYMPTOMS AND RUNS TESTS,
COLLECTS DATA BUT CANNOT
ANALYZE IT ON SITE

ENGINEER BRINGS DATA
TO LAB FOR FURTHER WORK

ENGINEER ANALYZES DATA
AND DEVELOPS HYPOTHESES
REGARDING SOURCE OF MISREADS

ENGINEER GOES TO THE PLANT
WITH NEW IDEAS TO TEST

ENGINEER RUNS TESTS,
CONFIRMS DIAGNOSIS, AND
MODIFIES SOFTWARE ON SITE
TO ADDRESS THE PROBLEM.

The majority of the adaptation events studied were also characterized by iteration between plant and lab (see Figure 2). In all but six cases, engineers had to go to the plant at some point in the problem solving process. And in almost all of these cases, engineers subsequently had to move back to the lab for more problem solving. In 40% of all cases, engineers moved between plant and lab three or more times. This is particularly significant since the decision to relocate problem solving was not a trivial one; each physical shift between the plant and the lab entailed two to three hours in driving time alone.

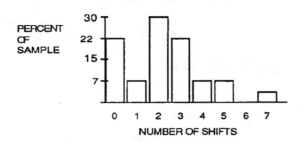

FIGURE 2

NUMBER OF SHIFTS BETWEEN PLANT AND
LAB DURING PROBLEM SOLVING

We next explored why problem solving activities were location-specific --
that is, what learning-related reasons did engineers have for relocating problem
solving as frequently as they did? As noted above, previous research by others
suggests that problem solvers would shift between settings in order to facilitate
collaboration with colleagues (users at the plant or technical colleagues at the
lab). We explored this possibility using the problem solving protocols.

We examined each problem-related visit to either the plant or the lab, and
we recorded the set of problem solving activities that occurred there. A set of
activities was classified as collaborative inquiry when there was evidence of
significant conversation between engineers and users (or between engineers and
their technical colleagues) relating to development of shared ideas or a shared
understanding of a problem or its solution (Argyris and Schon, 1978; Daft and
Lengel, 1986). This definition encompasses Galegher and Kraut's (1990:2) point
that "the essence [of collaborative inquiry] is that ideas grow out of conversations
among participants." Respondents described these interactions in terms of
discussion, negotiation, argument, and the exchange of ideas. When there was
evidence of interaction between engineers and users (or others) involving only

simple requests (e.g., "Please do x"), or statements of fact (e.g., "Misplacements are occurring with y frequency"), or directions (e.g., "The best way to do that is like this"), we did not code them as collaborative inquiry.

We discovered that collaborative inquiry did not account for all or even most of the shifts observed. Instead, engineers often moved from the lab to the plant (or vice-versa) because further progress required access to the physical setting for search, observation, experimentation, or direct manipulation of technologies and procedures (see Table 1). We coded moves between lab and plant as involving access to the physical setting when engineers' activities at the site consisted of direct physical manipulation (e.g., undertaking experiments or test procedures) or observations of equipment and procedures. In these cases, engineers described the investigation in terms such as "I tested...", "I noticed...", " I saw..." or "I tried...".[2]

TABLE 1: SITUATION, NOT COLLABORATION

	Frequency	Percent of all problem-related visits
I. Nature of Activities Performed at the Plant.		
(A) collaborative inquiry with user	2	3%
(B) engineer uses other aspects of the local setting; (collaborative inquiry is not significant)	33	54%
Total	35	57%
II. Nature of Activities Performed at the Lab		
(A) uses collaborative inquiry with colleagues	6	10%
(B) engineer uses other aspects of the local setting, (collaborative inquiry is not significant).	20	33%
Total	26	43%

2 One concern with our data might be that collaborative inquiry was present, but omitted from verbal reports because developers wished to portray themselves as solely responsible for all adaptations This does not appear to be the case, since users' descriptions of the adaptive process corroborated developers' versions

It should be noted that even when collaboration did not occur, users' contributions were often important. Users provided information about local requirements and operating practices, scheduled time for engineers to use the machines, produced test parts, and assessed part quality. Simply by using the equipment, they made it possible for engineers to observe normal patterns of machine use. Similarly, laboratory assistants operated analytical equipment, implemented solutions in hardware or software, ordered parts, etc. We considered these to be support activities, and did not classify them as collaboration.

Participants reported relocating problem solving activities between plant and lab a total of 61 times (or 2.3 times per problem). However, in only 13% of those instances did the activities undertaken during the visit involve collaborative inquiry with others (see Table 1). More frequently (87% of all visits), problem solving activities undertaken during a single visit to the plant or lab involved observing and experimenting with physical phenomena within that setting. Thus, it appears that many of the shifts between lab and plant were motivated by the need to locate problem solving activities in a specific setting, and not the need to collaborate with others.

In the next sections, we explore the reasons why the physical setting of adaptive activities was so important. We then investigate reasons for repeatedly shifting problem solving activities between different settings in the course of dealing with a single problem. Finally, we seek to integrate our findings with previous literature that emphasizes the need for face-to-face collaboration for problem solving and adaptation, but that downplays (or overlooks) the importance of other aspects of the physical setting.

The Importance of the Physical Setting

We identified several reasons why the physical setting of adaptive activities was often critical. First, engineers needed to be on site to identify clues about machine problems that were embedded in the artifacts, procedures, and occurrences of the plant and the lab. Second, engineers needed to collect specific information that could not feasibly be collected and transmitted by others. Third, engineers needed to use tools or resources located in a specific site; indeed engineers' skills consisted, in part, in knowing how to use such tools. Finally, the physical setting shaped engineers' interactions with others. For all these reasons, the skill that the engineer could display depended, in part, on where he or she was working. Below, we discuss these four issues in more detail

Knowledgeable action involves recognizing and using embedded clues.

Engineers brought technical knowledge of the machine to users' problems, however this knowledge was seldom sufficient to identify the source of users' complaints immediately. In only 2 of the 27 problems studied could engineers grasp the nature of the problem without some direct visual inspection (see appendix). Rather, engineers' deep technical knowledge enabled them to recognize when occurrences, patterns, or artifacts were anomalous, and therefore potentially informative "clues" to the underlying cause of the observed problem symptom. But this skill was necessarily situated: to discover a clue means to pick out as noteworthy some aspect of the specific setting that is not obvious to everyone.

Project participants recognized this. They repeatedly used the phrase, "you just had to be there." In describing one problem in the placement cell, the user explained, "We tried the telephone, the tube [electronic mail]....it was endless. You just had to be there and see it " The engineer agreed that "I just don't know what is going on until I see the problem. To look and know what I see is exactly what I get paid for!"

For example, in one case users had complained repeatedly that the placer machine was "drifting": placements were gradually wandering out of tolerance over time. The engineer tried to investigate the problem over the phone. Based on descriptions from the user, he surmised that users must be programming the machine incorrectly. Since users always assured him that they were doing this as instructed, progress was stymied. Finally the engineer went to the plant, and immediately noticed that two screws on the camera head had loosened. According to the engineer, "I saw it immediately and connected it with the drifting problem."

In this case, had the engineer simply asked users to check the screws, they could easily have collected the information he needed. The problem, of course, is that the engineer could not have predicted the relevance of the screws, but rather had to discover it. His reasoning was "guided by the characteristics of the evoking stimulus and by the momentary context" (Kahneman and Miller, 1986:150). Once the engineer went to the plant, there were many contextual cues to guide his attention to the loose screws. And once he noticed the loose screws, this one discovery "laid down a trace" (Schank, 1982) to help guide further exploration. That is, discovery of one clue prepared the engineer to notice other clues, or to take further exploratory action to find more clues. New clues could then be used to develop a richer and more precise explanation of the problem. Specifically, the engineer's discovery of the anomalous loose screws led him to pull other associations from memory (such as the reason he had used screws on the camera), to notice other clues in the plant environment (such as the maintenance procedures applied to the machine), and to revise previous assumptions (such as that screws were secure because they had been sealed with loctite).

This example also highlights why it matters <u>who</u> undertakes investigation in a given physical context. In this case, users were present in the plant throughout the process, and the screws were easily visible to anyone who looked. However, different people attend to different stimuli, depending on what is surprising or anomalous for them (Neisser, 1976). For users, important anomalies were any deviations from the smooth processing of high-quality parts. Thus they noticed characteristics of the misplacements (number, timing, seriousness), but did not notice characteristics of the machine itself. Since the machine was new to them, their expectations about how machine elements <u>should</u> appear were still vague and provided them with few opportunities to be surprised.

Accordingly, engineers often pointed out that users' observations were "too general" to be helpful. The engineer working on the placement cell, for example, complained that "what the operator will see is just 'it's not placing right'." For him, this was a very general statement because it could be caused by hundreds of different technical factors. However, for users, who attended to placement precision within one-onethousanth of an inch, this complaint was a highly specific statement of the situation.

The engineer, by contrast, approached the plant with very specific expectations about how the machine ought to look during operations -- even though he had no well-developed expectations about how the parts would look once completed. In the example above, the engineer specifically (although implicitly) expected that the camera head screws would be tight, and thus he had the capacity to be surprised by their looseness.

Moreover, the loose screws were noteworthy to the engineer because, given his knowledge of machine design, he could use this observation to construct an explanation about what was wrong with the machine. It is entirely possible that the user had at some time looked at the screws; however, since the user did not know enough about the machine's design to connect the screws to the machine problem, he would have assumed implicitly that they were not relevant. As the engineer explained, "The problem is not whether the data exists, but what constitutes data -- and the answer is different for me and for [the user]."

Like the plant, the lab also contained many clues to machine problems. In one instance, the engineer went first to the plant to examine a problem involving light reflection off the circuit board surface. He was not sure how to proceed next, and returned to the lab to consider the issue. When he got there he encountered a colleague from another company carrying a circuit board with a very different surface coating design. The engineer examined the new board and, as he explained, he gradually "began to see" how the alternative design could help to alleviate the reflection problem

In this example, the stimuli that lead the engineer to develop a new solution simply did not exist in the plant; on the other hand, any other engineer (who was not engaged in this particular problem) would probably not have noticed the new board as a surprising, noteworthy stimulus. The new board certainly would not have triggered other engineers to construct a vision of how the design could be useful, because they did not have the reflection problem in mind at the time.

Data-gathering skills are exploited in situ.

Another aspect of engineers' expertise was their skill in gathering relevant data. Sometimes, engineers knew what information they needed, but the information could not simply be collected by a local user and conveyed by mail or phone call or even by face-to-face discussion. As one of the engineers explained,

> The form of data [that the user] uses is different, and the scheme he uses to collect it is not always clear to me, so you cannot just [use] his data ... The data I am interested in, the plant guys may have very little incentive to collect or use. And gathering data is not at all straightforward, because the picture that the user sees on the screen is not the same as what the machine

sees

As this implies, noticing and gathering information involved considerable on-site interpretation (von Hippel, 1993). Thus, being on-site to observe and record events mattered to adaptation outcomes.

Knowledgeable Action Lies in the Ability to Use Local Tools and Resources

Engineers' skills also consisted, in part, in knowing how to use tools for gathering data (such as diagnostic software), for analyzing it (such as powerful computing resources) or for designing solutions (such as mechanical lab equipment). Since many of these tools were available only in a particular setting, this meant that engineers' abilities were partly dependent on the physical setting of the work. For example, engineers often had to go to the plant because they needed to use the diagnostic software routines embedded in the machine; at other times, they needed to go back to the lab to use specialized instruments (e.g. oscilloscopes, microscopes) located there.

It is important to note that engineers' ability to use specific tools constituted important aspects of their expertise. As Hutchins (1990) points out, tools and other physical artifacts do not just amplify people's cognitive skills, because considerable expertise is often needed to use them in the first place. Thus, "the act of getting into coordination with the artifact constitutes an expert performance by the person" (Hutchins, 1990:205-6). This was reflected in engineers' comments, such as the statement that "There is so much information in the machine [that] it takes a very specialized skill to absorb it."

Human interactions are embedded in the surrounding physical context

So far, we have argued that individual engineers' abilities to investigate and resolve problems was (partly) embedded in the physical settings where they worked. In addition, social interactions that contributed to problem solving were also embedded in their physical contexts. Aspects of the local setting could affect when interactions took place, and what they accomplished. At the same time, social interactions partly shaped the physical setting by illuminating events or objects that otherwise would have gone unnoticed.

An example comes from the case in which the engineer went to the plant to investigate a problem with the placer. After studying the problem in the plant and tracing it to light reflection, the engineer returned to the lab to work toward a solution. At the lab, he "happened to notice" a circuit board with a new surface coating design. This discovery, in turn, led the engineer to seek out a colleague who had designed the board, and to engage him in discussion. Moreover, discussion with his colleague illuminated aspects of the circuit board that the engineer had not perceived on his own. In other cases, when engineers went to the plant to investigate a problem, the physical clues they spotted triggered interaction with users (such as further questions about the symptoms observed). This often lead to discovery of further clues. Further, as engineer discovered additional clues or gathered more data, they were often better able to interpret users' comments and observations.

Interactions and discussions were also situated in the sense that local tools could be an integral part of the inquiry process. For example, in one case the engineer working on the profiler (who was an electrical engineer by training) brought a damaged machine component to the lab. She wanted to discuss possible causes for the failure with a mechanically-oriented colleague. Since much of the colleague's expertise lay in his talent for using the diagnostic equipment in his lab, this equipment and the opportunities for action embodied in the lab were central to their joint inquiry. In other cases, engineers' ability to make use of local tools or resources depended on opportunities to interact with the people at that site. For example, engineers could gain access to production equipment by going to the plant, but they lacked the skills to operate production processes or to evaluate their output. Thus, their ability to undertake sophisticated experiments often depended on access to users' production skills. Moreover, engineers sometimes had to seek out users' insights before they could interpret results or consider next steps.

Thus even when adaptive activities involved discussion and negotiation, these processes were not independent of their physical setting. The physical setting for group activities partly determined what capabilities the group brought to bear, what it could do, and what new insights group members would discover.

A Dynamic View of the Learning Process: Iteration Between Plant and Lab Settings

In the previous section we presented some reasons why engineers' ability to learn from errors was situated in *both* lab and plant. At the same time, it was also true that the "knowledge in" a particular setting (in the form of clues, or needed tools and resources, or relevant information) depended on the understanding that the engineer brought to it. Since the engineer's knowledge was not static, this meant that the "knowledge in" different settings changed over time. In many cases, an engineer could not do everything she needed to do in a single visit to the plant. She might not know enough to recognize embedded clues, or to take advantage of tools or information located in that setting. However, when her understanding of a particular problem evolved during a subsequent visit to the lab, she could then return to the plant to recognize previously-unnoticed clues or to make good use of previously-unused resources located there. This meant that there was an intimate and *dynamic* interaction between the "knowledge in" a particular setting and the understanding in the engineer's head.

Physically, this dynamic interaction shows up as a "zigzag" pattern in the location of problem solving. A good example is the case where users of the profiler complained that the machine's Y axis was "drifting". The engineer involved in that project had to relocate her investigation from plant to lab and back again seven different times before tracing the problem to a worn coupling inside the machine. (The process is described graphically in Figure 3.) As a physical matter, of course, the coupling was available in the plant throughout the period, and the engineer had always known how to disassemble the machine and how to recognize signs of wear. However, the engineer needed to undertake considerable investigation in both plant and lab before she learned enough to think of coupling wear as the source of the problem. Only at that point did the coupling begin to be a salient part of the plant environment in the engineer's eyes.

FIGURE 3: PHYSICAL SHIFTS IN SOLVING A COMPLEX PROBLEM

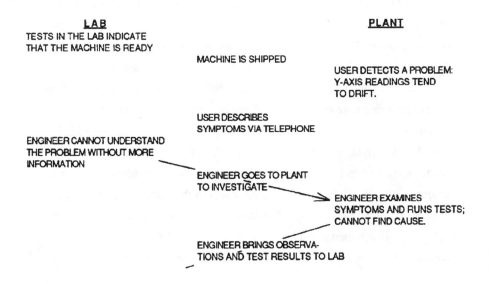

(FIGURE 3, CONTINUED)

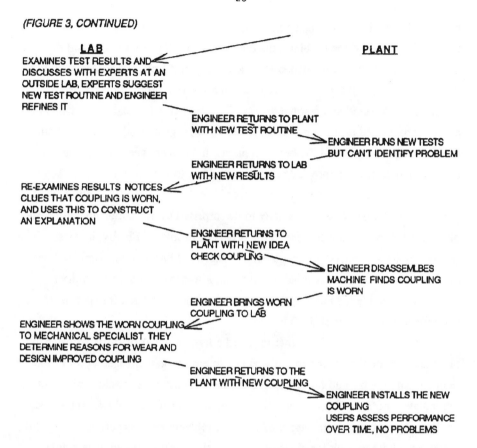

LAB
EXAMINES TEST RESULTS AND
DISCUSSES WITH EXPERTS AT AN
OUTSIDE LAB, EXPERTS SUGGEST
NEW TEST ROUTINE AND ENGINEER
REFINES IT

PLANT

ENGINEER RETURNS TO PLANT
WITH NEW TEST ROUTINE
ENGINEER RUNS NEW TESTS
BUT CAN'T IDENTIFY PROBLEM

ENGINEER RETURNS TO LAB
WITH NEW RESULTS

RE-EXAMINES RESULTS NOTICES
CLUES THAT COUPLING IS WORN,
AND USES THIS TO CONSTRUCT
AN EXPLANATION

ENGINEER RETURNS TO
PLANT WITH NEW IDEA
CHECK COUPLING
ENGINEER DISASSEMLBES
MACHINE FINDS COUPLING
IS WORN

ENGINEER BRINGS WORN
COUPLING TO LAB

ENGINEER SHOWS THE WORN COUPLING
TO MECHANICAL SPECIALIST THEY
DETERMINE REASONS FOR WEAR AND
DESIGN IMPROVED COUPLING

ENGINEER RETURNS TO THE
PLANT WITH NEW COUPLING
ENGINEER INSTALLS THE NEW
COUPLING
USERS ASSESS PERFORMANCE
OVER TIME, NO PROBLEMS

This case is an extreme one, but multiple shifts among sites were common. We noted above (see Figure 2) that repeated, iterative working sessions in the plant and the lab were required in approximately two-thirds of all problems encountered.

The problems that demanded a larger number of iterations between plant and lab were not necessarily more difficult or complex than those requiring fewer "zig-zag" relocations. Instead, whether the engineer could interpret the problem satisfactorily during a single visit to the plant depended on the links among the nature of the problem, the engineer's existing knowledge, and the clues and resources that happened to be available in the plant. Problems could be diagnosed on an initial plant visit only when all of the information and tools needed to understand and resolve the problem resided in the plant, *and* when the engineer happened to bring the background knowledge needed to exploit them. In some cases, very few shifts between plant and lab were needed because the engineer's background knowledge predisposed her to look just where the key clues lay. Also, in these cases the engineer brought a sufficiently explicit set of expectations that she had the capacity to be surprised by any subtle anomalies she discovered, and to connect these to the observed problem. Finally, in cases where few relocations occurred, the engineers' background knowledge, combined with the tools and resources available in the plant, also provided her the ability to select and implement an appropriate response without the need for special equipment or resources at the lab.

In the case of problems that required a large number of shifts between plant and lab, on the other hand, it was not so easy to gather together all of the requisite knowledge and resources in one place. In these cases, clues were not immediately noticeable, even when engineers examined the problem in the plant context. Unless engineers happened to bring relevant prior experience, they did not know where to look for clues on a first visit -- or they failed to recognize clues that they did encounter. Therefore, engineers needed first to gather other kinds of clues or information embedded in a different environment -- the lab. In addition, engineers often needed to use specialized tools located in the plant during one phase of the problem solving process, and to use tools located in the lab as they progressed to another phase (or vice-versa). Thus, as engineers made discoveries or collected data in one site, they became better able to exploit the "knowledge in" another setting. This explains why, in most of the cases studied, skillful adaptive activity entailed moving between different physical settings in a repeated, iterative pattern.

DISCUSSION

This paper has examined one example of adaptive learning processes in organizations: responding to technical problems with new process machinery. We find that adaptive learning is often highly situated. That is, the ability to understand and resolve problems is only partly located in experts' heads. It is also located in the experts' ability to recognize and to enact clues about the problem or its solution. Typically, these clues are embedded in the everyday practices and particular experiences of specific organizational settings. Adaptive learning is also situated in that it depends on experts' ability to utilize resources and to gather information that are embedded in particular physical settings. Thus, to understand and resolve problems, experts need to make use of the practices, occurrences, beliefs, and artifacts available in specific, concrete settings.

The notion of situated learning has been discussed by other authors in the literature on learning (e.g., Lave, 1984; Scribner, 1984; Suchman, 1987) and organizations (e.g. Brown and Duguid, 1991; Pentland, 1992). However we build on the concept by showing that the learning process may be situated in multiple organizational settings, and not just one. Very often, a problem in one setting can be understood only by moving to a different setting. Indeed, problem solvers may need to move in an iterative fashion between settings because, as they gain knowledge in (and about) one setting, they become better able to recognize and use the knowledge in (and about) another setting or location. In effect, by relocating problem solving activities, learners change the structure of the problem, the options for action, and the knowledge they can act upon.

This finding adds a new dimension to traditional theories of learning and problem solving. Simon (1981:153) has suggested that "solving a problem simply means representing it so as to make the solution transparent." Typically, we might think of representational choices in terms of mental frameworks, two-dimensional pictures or diagrams, or physical or computational models. Organizational theorists have added that who is involved in the investigation -- in terms of functional or demographic characteristics -- helps to frame the problem (e.g. Katz, 1982). In this work, we suggest that problems often look different if seen from different physical locations. This is not only because different sites provide a different view in the literal sense, but also because different sites embody the potential for different kinds of informed discovery and knowledgeable action.

It is interesting to compare these findings to previous work that emphasizes the collaborative or interpersonal nature of adaptive learning processes in organizations (Argyris and Schon, 1978; Cicourel, 1990; Brown and Duguid, 1991). We suggest that our emphasis on the importance of the physical setting adds an additional dimension to this literature. First, we find that collaboration with others is only one way for individuals to gain new insights about a problem. Relocating problem solving activities is also important, because the physical setting partly determines what kinds of skills and expertise an individual can bring to bear on a given problem. Moreover, even when collaborative inquiry does occur, the insights produced are often influenced by their physical setting. The stimuli, distractions, resources, and pressures present in a given setting can all influence the group's opportunities for knowledgeable interaction and discovery. Since problems seldom have a single "right" answer or interpretation, it may be important to acknowledge that the way problems get resolved, and the lessons that are drawn from them, are not independent of where problem solving occurs.

Throughout this work, our focus had been on adaptive learning in response to one class of problems -- those affecting new process equipment. Yet our findings may be generalizable to many other kinds of adaptive learning situations. In our research, the place where problems occurred (the context of use) was physically distinct from where problem solvers were located (the lab, or context of design). This separation is common to many realms of organizational activity besides machine design. Strategic decision making, product development, software system configuration, medical treatment, and executive education all take place in very different settings from the ones where the resulting policies or technologies are actually put into practice. These different settings embody the possibility for different sorts of action and discovery. Indeed, it is a characteristic of complex organizations that knowledge, activities, and resources are distributed -- not only among people with different specialized competencies, but also among multiple physical settings. Thus, we would expect to see considerable iteration between these different settings when problems arise with new technologies or managerial policies.

Even for activities that have traditionally been considered "context-free", such as scientific research, the physical and social context of the work can significantly affect learning processes and outcomes (Woolgar and Latour, 1979; Lave, 1984). Thus, our findings may be applicable even when we are not considering the transition of new technologies (or policies) from design to use. For example, we know that research engineers often seek input from technical colleagues in other functions or organizations (Allen, 1977). Our findings suggest that they are likely to hold different conversations and to learn different things depending on whether these interactions take place in the R&D lab, or outside, or both.

These ideas have important managerial implications. Based on the popular management literature, many managers form the impression that the way to support learning is to gather together the right project team and to encourage intensive collaboration. The need for co-location is widely emphasized. However, the importance of the location itself is often not taken into account. By contrast, our work suggests that it matters greatly *where* such a team performs its work. The knowledge that team members can bring to bear, and the kinds of informed search and discovery they can engage in, will be determined in part by the physical setting where they come together. Moreover, our research suggests that any one physical setting may fail to provide all of the clues and resources needed to fully exploit the expertise within such a group. Managers need to consider not only who talks to whom, but also where such interactions occur, and how to enable iteration between different settings. Unfortunately, corporate policies that encourage face-to-face interactions do not always enable problem solvers to move freely between different settings in pursuit of deeper understanding about problems and their causes.

These issues should be familiar to organizational scientists, most of whom spend their careers moving back-and-forth between the field and their university offices. Yet, the situated process of adaptive learning in different organizational settings has seldom been closely studied. If it is indeed central to the process of adaptive learning, it merits further research.

REFERENCES

Allen, T.J. (1977) Making the Flow of Technology Cambridge, MA: MIT Press.

Argyris, C. & Schon, D. (1978) Organizational Learning. Reading, MA: Addison Wesley.

Brown, J.S. & Duguid, P. (1991) "Organizational Learning and Communities-of-Practice: Toward a Unified View of Working, Learning and Innovation." Organization Science, Vol. 2, No. 1, 40-57.

Ching, C., Holsapple, C.W. and Whinston, A.B. (1992) "Reputation, Learning and Coordination in Distributed Decision-Making Contexts." Organization Science, Vol. 3, No. 2, 275-297.

Cicourel, A. (1990) "The Integration of Distributed Knowledge in Collaborative Medical Diagnosis." In J. Galegher, R. Kraut, & C. Egido (Eds.) Intellectual Teamwork: Social and Technological Foundations of Cooperative Work, Hillsdale, NJ: Lawrence Erlbaum Associates, Publishers.

Daft, R. & Lengel, R. (1986) "Organizational Information Requirements, Media Richness and Structural Design." Management Science, Vol. 32, No. 5, 554-571.

Fiol, C.M. & Lyles, M. (1985) "Organizational Learning." Academy of Management Review, Vol. 10, No. 4, 803-813.

Galegher, J., Kraut, R., & Egido, C. (1990) Intellectual Teamwork: Social and Technological Foundations of Cooperative Work. Hillsdale, NJ: Lawrence Erlbaum Associates, Publishers.

Hedberg, B. (1981) "How Organizations Learn and Unlearn." In P. C. Nystrom & W. Starbuck (Eds.) Handbook of Organizational Design, Vol. 2. Oxford, England: Oxford University Press. 3-26.

Hutchins, E. (1990) "The Technology of Team Navigation." In J. Galegher, R. Kraut, & C. Egido (Eds.) Intellectual Teamwork: Social and Technological Foundations of Cooperative Work. Hillsdale, NJ: Lawrence Erlbaum Associates, Publishers.

Kahneman, D. & Miller, D. (1986) "Norm Theory: Comparing Reality to Its Alternatives." Psychological Review, Vol. 93, No. 2, 136-153.

Katz, R. (1982) "The Effects of Group Longevity on Project Communication and Performance." Administrative Science Quarterly, Vol. 27, 81-104.

Latour, B. & Woolgar, S. 1(979) Laboratory Life: The Social Construction of Scientific Facts. Beverly Hills, CA: Sage Publications.

Lave, J. (1988) Cognition in Practice: Mind, Mathematics, and Culture in Everyday Life. New York: Cambridge University Press.

Lave, J.,Murtaugh, M. and de la Rocha, O. (1984) "The Dialectic of Arithmetic in Grocery Shopping." In B. Rogoff & J. Lave (Eds.) Everyday Cognition: Its Development in Social Context. Cambridge, MA: Harvard University Press.

Leonard-Barton, D. (1988) "Implementation as Mutual Adaptation of Technology and Organization." Research Policy, 17, 251-267.

Leonard-Barton, D. (1991) "Inanimate Integrators: A Block of Wood Speaks." Design Management Journal, Vol. 2, No. 3.

Levinthal, D. & March, J. (1981) "A Model of Adaptive Organizational Search." Journal of Economic Behavior and Organization, Vol. 2, 307-333.

Levitt, B. & March, J. (1988) "Organizational Learning." Annual Review of Sociology, Vol. 14, 31-40.

Lounamaa, P. & March, J. (1987) "Adaptive Coordination of a Learning Team." Management Science. Vol. 33, No. 1, 107-123.

March, J. & Olsen, J. (1975) "The Uncertainty of the Past: Organizational Learning under Ambiguity," European Journal of Political Research, Vol. 3, 147-171.

Neisser, U. (1976) Cognition and Reality. San Francisco: W. H. Freeman.

Pentland, B. (1992) "Organizing Moves in Software Support Hot Lines." Administrative Science Quarterly, Vol. 37, 527-548.

Rosenberg, N. (1982) Inside the Black Box, Cambridge: Cambridge Univ. Press.

Rogoff, B. (1984) "Thinking and Learning in Social Context." In B. Rogoff & J. Lave (Eds.) Everyday Cognition: Its Development in Social Context. Cambridge, MA: Harvard University Press.

Schank, R. C. (1982) Dynamic Memory: Learning in Computers and People. New York: Cambridge University Press.

Schon, D. & Wiggins, G. (1992) "Kinds of Seeing and Their Functions in Designing." Design Studies, Vol. 13, No. 2, 135-156.

Scribner, S. 1984, "Studying Working Intelligence." In B. Rogoff & J. Lave (Eds.) Everyday Cognition: Its Development in Social Context. Cambridge, MA: Harvard University Press.

Simon, H. (1981) The Sciences of the Artificial. Cambridge, MA: MIT Press.

Suchman, L. (1987) Plans and Situated Actions: The Problem of Human Machine Communication. New York. Cambridge University Press.

Tyre, M.J. & Hauptman, O. (1992) "Effectiveness of Organizational Responses to Technological Change in the Production Process." Organization Science, Vol. 3, No. 3, 301-315.

Van de Ven, A., Angle, H., and Poole, M.S. (1989) Research on the Management of Innovation. New York: Harper and Row, Ballinger Division.

Van de Ven, A. and Polley, D. (1992) "Learning while Innovating." Organization Science, Vol 3, N. 1, 92-116.

von Hippel, E. (1993) "The Impact of 'Sticky Information' on Innovation and Problem Solving." Forthcoming in Management Science.

Weick, K. (1979) The Social Psychology of Organizing, second edition. New York: Random House.

Zaltman, G., Duncan, R.B., and Holbek, J. (1973) Innovation in Organizations. New York. John Wiley and Sons.

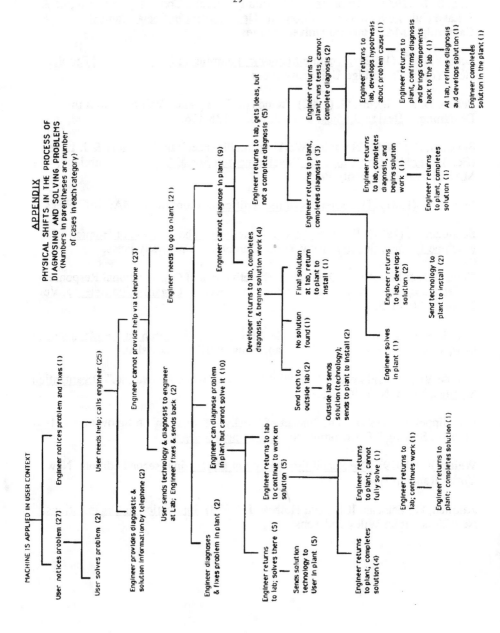

APPENDIX

PHYSICAL SHIFTS IN THE PROCESS OF
DIAGNOSING AND SOLVING PROBLEMS
(Numbers in parentheses are number
of cases in each category)

The *International Center for Research on the Management of Technology*
Sloan School of Management
Massachusetts Institute of Technology

Working Paper and Reprint List

Number Date	Title	Author(s)
1-89 11/89	Netgraphs: A Graphic Representation of Adjacency Tool for Matrices as a Network Analysis	George Allen
2-90 8/89	Strategic Transformation and the Success of High Technology Companies	Roberts
3-90 1/90 (Rev. 3/91)	Managing CAD Systems in Mechanical Design Engineering	Robertson Allen
4-90 1/90	The Personality and Motivations of Technological Entrepreneurs	Roberts
5-90 4/90	Current Status and Future of Structural Panels in the Wood Products Industry	Montrey Utterback
6-90R 8/92	Do Nominated Boundary Spanners Become Effective Technological Gatekeepers?	Allen Nochur
7-90 7/90	The Treble Ladder Revisited: Why Do Engineers Lose Interest in the Dual Ladder as They Grow Older?	Allen Katz
8-90 8/90	Technological Discontinuities: The Emergence of Fiber Optics	McCormack Utterback
9-90 8/90	Work Environment, Organizational Relationships and Advancement of Technical Professionals: A Ten Year Longitudinal Study in One Organization	Basa Allen Katz
10-90 8/90	People and Technology Transfer	Allen
11-90 8/90	Exploring the Dynamics of Dual Ladders: A Longitudinal Study	Katz Tushman Allen
12-90 8/90	Managing the Introduction of New Process Technology: International Differences in a Multi-Plant Network	Tyre
13-90 8/90	Task Characteristics and Organizational Problem Solving in Technological Process Change	Tyre
14-90 8/90	The Impact of 'Sticky Data' on Innovation and Problem-Solving	von Hippel
15-90 5/90	Underinvestment and Incompetence as Responses to Radical Innovation: Evidence from the Photolithographic Alignment Equipment Industry	Henderson
16-90 7/90	Patterns of Communication Among Marketing, Engineering and Manufacturing — A Comparison Between Two New Product Teams	Griffin Hauser

Paper numbers with the suffix R are reprints

The International Center for Research on the Management of Technology

Working Paper Order Form

Name: _____

Title: _____

Company:_____

Address: _____

_____

_____

☐ I would like to become a working paper subscriber and receive all papers published during the current year. ($150 U.S., Canada, Mexico; $175 all other countries)

☐ I would like to order working papers individually. Please send me the following papers:

_____   # _____   # _____

_____   # _____   # _____

_____   # _____   # _____

Total number papers ordered _____ @ $9.00/paper $_____

Additional postage charges $_____
(shipments outside US only)

Subscription rate $_____

Total Due $_____

Within the US: All orders mailed first class.
Outside the US: For orders to Canada add $.15 per paper for air delivery. For orders to other countries, add $.25 per paper for surface delivery or $2.00 per paper for air delivery.

PAYMENT MUST ACCOMPANY THIS ORDER

Make check or money order (in US funds) payable to:

MIT / ICRMOT

and send to: ICRMOT Working Papers
MIT, Room E56-390
Cambridge MA 02139-4307

57.

CPSIA information can be obtained
at www.ICGtesting.com
Printed in the USA
LVHW080544280623
750924LV00011B/1481